God
Is Interested
In You

Adeoye Oyewo

Foreword By Ven. Prof. Adedayo Ejiwunmi

Halo
PUBLISHING
INTERNATIONAL

ISBN: 978-1-61244-714-8
Library of Congress Control Number: 2018965527

Printed in the United States of America

Halo Publishing International
1100 NW Loop 410
Suite 700 - 176
San Antonio, Texas 78213
1-877-705-9647
www.halopublishing.com
contact@halopublishing.com

To the memory of Oluremi and Adejoke Fatikun

Acknowledgments

The whole idea of putting together these divinely inspired words started in November of 2016. At that time, I was led to begin an online evangelical platform, along with my partners, to support an already existing ministry. The contents of this book represent God's way of reaching mankind because of His deep love for us and the interest He has in our lives. I give glory to God for He alone has sent His messages and granted me the enablement to communicate them to show that He is genuinely interested in us. I would also like to acknowledge the many persons who have played critical roles in my spiritual growth without whom use could not have been found for me in God's vineyard. They are too numerous, but permit me to mention Reverend Dr. and Reverend Mrs. Samuel Adeleye and Reverend Dr. Aderemi Fakorede. I must also not fail to appreciate my parents, Deacon John Adebayo Oyewo and the late Mrs. Maria Omowunmi Oyewo who, having received help from God, invested so much in my early life to give me a solid Christian foundation. My sincere appreciation and gratitude go to my wife, Christine, who has been by my side all the way. She is a helper good enough for me. To my great treasures, EbunOluwa and Oluwamiwunmi, for continuing in their excellent counsel and support; I appreciate you both. To the Venerable Professor Adedayo B. Ejiwunmi, who has found time to read the manuscripts and write the foreword: I am deeply indebted and cannot thank him enough.

Finally, last but not least, is my aunt, friend, and confidant, the Reverend Mrs. Bolanle Oyewo, who went through the content of this book in advance of publication; may you remain blessed in Jesus' name.

> *"This Vision is for a future time. It describes the end, and it will be fulfilled. If it seems slow in coming, wait patiently, for it will surely take place. It will not be delayed."*
>
> *(Habakkuk 2:3 NLT)*

Adeoye Oyewo
Lagos, Nigeria
September, 2018

Contents

Foreword

When one sees the passion and the purpose behind a project, one must commend the effort and commitment that turns the dream into reality. It does not always happen. It is one thing to feel strongly about something; it is another to think and work through the process that changes the feeling into concrete achievement. This book is a dream realized. It pulsates with the author's sincere love for God and his deep concern for every fellow human being, especially those who have not, as Jesus said, "heard or seen or touched the word of life." The author is very anxious that such people should share in that fullness of joy which Jesus promises to those who turn to Him with a genuine change of mind and simple trust in His love and power. Fortunately, for the reader's benefit, the author has written from his many personal experiences of God's intimate interest and achievements in his own life.

Three main thoughts preoccupied the mind of the author as he wrote this collection of brief talks. You might call them tracts. The first is the seriousness of sin. Heavily influenced by current Western thinking, the concept of sin is fast losing value, relevance, and conviction. Thank God that no matter how many versions of the Bible we may have, the reality of the guilty conscience and being morally accountable to God cannot be erased from experience and Scriptures. God is holy and therefore angry about our falling short of His glory. He is lovingly interested enough in every human being not to let him perish in hell–the final home prepared not for man but Satan.

The second preoccupation is the sufficiency of Jesus Christ as the complete satisfactory provision given by God for the forgiveness of sin and the restoration of every man to God. In this book, the once-for-all "foolish" sacrifice of Jesus is shown over and over again to be the greatest wisdom for the calamity in which man has found himself. This rescue is not only full, but it is also free. That is the degree of interest God has in us.

The third preoccupation is the reality of death. Many of these tracts make that point clearly and soberly from Biblical stories and our daily observations. I often think it is an insult to one's intellectual awareness to be reminded of the inevitability of death. Living carelessly as if one is ignorant of the fact must be a great intentional self-deceit or Satan-induced forgetfulness and arrogance. In view of the obvious, the author has labored to show that a correct relationship with Jesus is the only way to prepare for death and hence eternity. For this, the author wants all men to know that God has always been and is still so interested in every individual that He wants everyone to be saved and to receive rich rewards in heaven by serving "Him in holiness and righteousness all the days of their lives" on earth.

I recommend this book strongly for the following reasons. Firstly, it is a book that can be used as a devotional, especially for young converts. One tract a day will enhance that crucial decision to be a follower of Jesus. It will also be a good motivation to early evangelistic activity.

Secondly, still on evangelism, each tract can be photocopied for particular persons, as may be appropriate for his spiritual need. That may be a good way to follow up.

Sincerely a good number of tracts can come out of this publication and therefore reach a wider audience.

Finally, I thank the author very much for asking me to write the foreword. I have benefitted a great deal from some particular Bible references which I had not taken seriously. I am sure its simple, direct, and practical presentations will enrich the lives of both young and old and challenge us all to get out of our complacent mode.

Ven. Prof. Adedayo B. Ejiwunmi
Lagos, Nigeria
October, 2018

Preface

The fact that our lives are important to God is never in doubt. Notwithstanding man's misdemeanors, God was never willing to give up on man having created him in His image. Although the world is inhabited by many who are not committed to the Almighty and His ways, it has always been clear that God's commitment to His most preferred and loved creation is unwavering and eternal. The proof of His commitment, the purpose of which is to save man from eternal condemnation, was exemplified by the sending of His Son to make the ultimate sacrifice for man. Jesus paid the full price for our redemption as proof of His father's love for us. As part of the package, God also sent us the Holy Spirit to abide with us and so guide our daily walk with Him. Unfortunately, the battle for the soul of man which started in the Garden of Eden continues unabated. This battle is fought on a daily basis in the lives of all humans and will only cease at the second coming of Jesus. This book entitled "God Is Interested in You" provides guidance on your daily living to help you overcome the wiles of the wicked one. It defines God's expectations from you in several short Gospel-centered messages. You must, therefore, take charge of your life so that you do not fall prey to the one who "has come to kill, steal and destroy" (John 10:10). He is going about "like a roaring lion looking for someone to devour" (1 Peter 5:8). You must not allow him to ruin your life. The story below, narrated by Bro Gbile Akanni, typifies the struggle that man faces and is entitled "Don't Make a Wrong Choice." It goes thus:

> While in our youth days, after our graduation from the university, we were posted for service. A vibrant Christian brother and I reported to our service center. Not long after our arrival, some people organized a welcome party for NYSC (Corpers), where we were both invited. Immediately, I said, "No, we're God's children; we don't attend worldly parties."
>
> They replied, "You are S.U., you are old-school, you are suegbe" (which translates as uncivilized).
>
> At this junction, my friend couldn't take a stand for the Lord. He made a choice. He said to me, Bro Gbile, please let's not do so; let's attend. It's just a party; nothing more. But I insisted on my decision.
>
> So, he honored their invitation. According to him, seated at the dancing hall, he was offered a bottle of alcohol. He rejected it and demanded a bottle of malt. While he was drinking, a lady walked up to him and said, "How can you, a man, be drinking malt? Even me, a girl, could

finish a bottle of Gulder." He became ashamed. For the first time in his life, he requested a glass of alcohol. To shorten the long tragic story, just a glass of beer took him away from Christ. Every effort l made to restore him to the faith was to no avail.

Many years later, l saw him, and hardly could l recognize him. He was so haggard and battered. His life was a mirage. His marriage was ruined, and his destiny was shattered. Then he looked at my face and said, "Bro Gbile, l envy you. What you are now is what l could have been, but look at where l am today. I wish l could reverse the choice l made." Then he stood weeping profusely. Though l prayed and restored him to Christ, the lost ground and the wasted years he never recovered. Not too long after, he died.

I believe this is why the Holy Spirit has strongly laid it on my heart to reach young people. Though your destiny is precious and very bright, it is contested. The ground the devil wins in your life today is where he will pitch his tent tomorrow. Now l see Jesus, the mighty warrior, with all His power and might ready to save you, but it seems the enemy is saying, "You are old enough to choose for yourself." The choice to win or lose is yours. To be victorious in the battle for the young, you must accept Jesus into your heart when you are young. As we read in Deuteronomy 30:19, "This day I call the heavens and the earth as witnesses against you that I have set before you life and death, blessings and curses. Now choose life, so that you and your children may live. Not about you only, but your children as well."

While God's desire is for you to have life abundant, the devil wants to destroy your destiny. Every day, you are faced with the choice of following God's way or the way of the world. Please endeavor to go with God. My prayer is that God will minister to you as you go through this book and that you will receive the power provided for you to live your life for Him.

God is genuinely interested in you. Do not take His love for granted.

Adeoye Oyewo
Lagos, Nigeria
September 2018

Chapter One

Great Is Thy Faithfulness

"The faithful love of the Lord never ends! His mercies never cease. Great is His faithfulness; His mercies begin afresh each morning. I say to myself, 'The Lord is my inheritance; therefore, I will hope in Him'"

(Lamentations 3:22–24 NLT)

God made all His creation beautiful and perfect. Unfortunately, sin came into the world through Adam and Eve leading to our being cut off from Him. The devil is today laughing at man; he is our number one enemy. Sexual immorality is the order of the day as man uses his body as he pleases, not minding the laws of God.

"Jerusalem, once so full of people, is now deserted. She, who was once great among the nations, now sits alone like a widow. Once the queen of all the earth, she is now a slave"

(Lamentations 1:1 NLT)

The consequences of sin are there for all to see. Man is rejected by his creator, and he continues to suffer all manner of troubles. There is pain, disgrace, immense suffering, and no help in sight. No one is spared God's anger and wrath. There is no hiding place for all.

"Jerusalem has sinned greatly, so she has been tossed away like a filthy rag. All who once honored her now despise her, for they have seen her stripped naked and humiliated. All she can do is groan and hide her face. She defiled herself with immorality and gave no thought to her future. Now she lies in the gutter with no one to lift her out. 'Lord, see my misery,' she cries. 'The enemy has triumphed.'"

(Lamentations 1:8–9 NLT)

You must do everything within your power to avoid God's anger. At all cost, this must be your goal. No one is God's equal, and in every situation, you are better off with God on your side. God's annoyance can make Him abandon you. Can a man contend with his creator?

"The Lord in His anger has cast a dark shadow over beautiful Jerusalem. The fairest of Israel's cities lies in the dust, thrown down from the heights of heaven. In His day of great anger, the Lord has shown no mercy even to His Temple. Without mercy, the Lord has destroyed every home in Israel. In His anger, He has broken down the fortress walls of beautiful Jerusalem. He has brought them to the ground, dishonoring the kingdom and its rulers"

(Lamentations 2:1–2 NLT)

Abandonment by God can lead to dire consequences. Sorrow permeates your life when God leaves you due to sin. Only repentance and the embrace of truth can save you.

"The people who once ate the richest foods now beg in the streets for anything they can get. Those who once wore the finest clothes now search the garbage dumps for food. The guilt of my people is greater than that of Sodom, where utter disaster struck in a moment, and no hand offered help"

(Lamentations 4:5–6 NLT)

Notwithstanding all these, God is faithful and ready to take us back anytime we turn to Him in true repentance. Thomas Chisholm wrote the song "Great Is Thy Faithfulness" as a testament to God's faithfulness through his very ordinary life. Born in a log cabin in Franklin, Kentucky, Chisholm became a Christian when he was twenty-seven and entered the ministry when he was thirty-six, though poor health forced him to retire after just one year. Chisholm explained toward the end of his life, "My income has not been large at any time due to impaired health in the earlier years, which has followed me on until now. Although I must not fail to record here the unfailing faithfulness of a covenant-keeping God and that He has given me many wonderful displays of His providing care, for which I am filled with astonishing gratefulness."

Just think, with each new day, God gives us the chance to prove His faithfulness. And throughout history, He's never once been proven wrong, for His mercies are new every morning, no matter what. (Excerpts from Gaither Homecoming Bible).

God Is Interested in You

You, too, can tap into the faithfulness and mercy of God, no matter your situation, circumstance, or what you have done wrong. Turn to Him today. There is hope in Him for you.

Chapter Two

Ekwueme

Our God is truly awesome. There is none like Him. What He says He will do; He is Someone who says something and does it. He matches His words with action.

I attended a unique praise programme on Saturday, January 20, 2018, and it was an extraordinary experience. The presence of God was manifested to me in a way unprecedented in recent times. It was an excellent meeting of God's children freely worshipping Him unhindered. I was so deeply moved and taken over that the two and a half hours spent in His presence just sped by without me noticing it.

One of the most powerful and inspiring worship songs that was rendered during the programme was titled "Ekwueme." I had never heard the song before and did not at that time know the meaning of the word, which is in the Igbo language (Igbo is one of the major Nigerian languages.) I do, however, remember that many of us just "'lost" ourselves in the presence of God when this song was being rendered. It was proof that God, indeed, inhabits the praise of His children.

Ekwueme means "fulfiller of promise." God is undoubtedly a fulfiller of all His promises.

"All right then, the Lord Himself will give you the sign. Look! The virgin will conceive a child! She will give birth to a son and will call Him Immanuel (which means 'God is with us')"

(Isaiah 7:14 NLT)

God sent His son Jesus to the world as promised. His virgin mother Mary gave birth to Him in a little town called Bethlehem.

"He was despised and rejected—a man of sorrows, acquainted with deepest grief. We turned our backs on Him and looked the other way. He was despised, and we did not care. Yet it was our weaknesses He carried; it was our sorrows that weighed Him down. And we thought His troubles were a punishment from God, a punishment for His own sins! But He was pierced for our rebellion, crushed for our sins. He was beaten so we could be whole. He was whipped so we could be healed. All of us, like sheep, have strayed away. We have left God's paths to follow our own. Yet the Lord laid on Him the sins of us all. He was oppressed and treated harshly, yet He never said a word. He was led like a lamb to the slaughter. And as a sheep is silent before the shearers, He did not open His mouth. Unjustly condemned, He was led away. No one cared that He died without descendants, that His life was cut short in midstream. But He was struck down for the rebellion of my people"

(Isaiah 53:3-8 NLT)

God delivered on His promise to offer man a salvation package that is adequate and made possible by the death and resurrection of His only begotten son Jesus Christ.

> *"'Men of Galilee," they said, "why are you standing here staring into heaven? Jesus has been taken from you into heaven, but someday He will return from heaven in the same way you saw him go!'"*
>
> *(Acts 1:11 NLT)*

God spoke again through His angelic vessels that Jesus is coming back again, and this time it is not as a lamb but as a judge. It is a promise you can choose to believe and so prepare for or disbelieve and so continue to ignore. The truth is that you can reject or turn down the offer of salvation, or even reconciliation, but you cannot reject the judgment of God when it comes through Christ Jesus on the last day. The contention here is between investing in life on earth and investing in eternal life; where will you pitch your tent? I pray that you will be wise to choose to invest in eternal life. God bless you.

> *"Let the one who is doing harm continue to do harm; let the one who is vile continue to be vile; let the one who is righteous continue to live righteously; let the one who is holy continue to be holy. Look, I am coming soon, bringing my reward with me to repay all people according to their deeds. I am the Alpha and the Omega, the First and the Last, the Beginning and the End"*
>
> *(Revelation 22:11–13 NLT)*

Chapter Three

God Wants You To Love, Not To Be In Love

"Dear friends, let us continue to love one another, for love comes from God. Anyone who loves is a child of God and knows God. But anyone who does not love does not know God, for God is love"

(1 John 4:7–8 NLT)

I once met a 28-year-old Irish man at the Hotel Sofitel Cairo Nile El Gezirah, and we engaged ourselves in some talk. Along the way, he digressed into his family life and told me his parents, though divorced, were still the best of friends. According to him, not a single day passes without them talking on the phone or seeing each other, as they both live in Dublin. I wondered why they were divorced, and he told me the reason was that they were no longer IN LOVE WITH EACH OTHER. I reflected deeply on this, and I consequently felt led to share the truth about matrimony.

"And He said, 'This explains why a man leaves his father and mother and is joined to his wife, and the two are united into one.' Since they are no longer two but one, let no one split apart what God has joined together"

(Matthew 19:5–6 NLT)

24

The concept of being in love today and being out of love tomorrow is at complete variance with God's words and His expectation. The union that is set up at marriage is indissoluble and should never be broken. Anything that is done to reverse it stands in contention with God's position. The basis of love is spiritual, as it comes from God. Being in love, on the other hand, is physical; it is a creation of man, and it cannot last.

Marriage is a relationship between three people, the third being God Himself who stands as a witness to the vows made by the couple. God is the architect of marriage and the only person who can add two entities and make them into one. He expects that in this union, both parties must recognize His presence always and give reverence to Him in their thoughts and deeds. The two must submit to each other in deference to Him and make sure that everything about their conduct within the union is with the mindset that God is watching every detail of their daily life.

> *"And further, submit to one another out of reverence for Christ"*
>
> *(Ephesians 5: 21 NLT)*

The oneness mystery of marriage is epitomized by the relationship between Christ and the Church. It is an unbreakable bond which does not allow for love transition: being in love today and out of love tomorrow. This love is irreversible and permanent. It is permitted only to come to an end at the cessation of life.

God's love is the centerpiece of marriage. The submission "as unto the Lord" demanded from the woman must be driven by love. The woman in the marriage structure is like the church while the man is like Christ. The love that the Church has for Christ, and which drives its submission, is as a result of His salvation gift. This love inspired-submission is a continuum. The woman must never go in and out of submission mode.

The love that Christ has for the Church, which defines God's expectation of man in this union, is unequivocal. It never changes. This means that a man must love his wife no matter what, and he must never fall in and out of love with her. This God kind of love does not allow for rejection excuses. It only recognizes the need to qualify the "faulty" wife the way Jesus qualified the Church to make it acceptable to Himself. A man never falls out of love with himself, so he must love his wife in perpetuity.

> *"For husbands, this means love your wives, just as Christ loved the church. He gave up His life for her to make her holy and clean, washed by the cleansing of God's word. He did this to present her to Himself as a glorious church without a spot or wrinkle or any other blemish. Instead, she will be holy and without fault"*
>
> *(Ephesians 5:25–27 NLT)*

God is unchangeable. God's love is therefore unchangeable. Being in love with each other is not part of His agenda for His children. God demands ONLY that we love one another. Any other form of love is not from Him and MUST be rejected.

I pray that God will reveal the truth about love to us and teach us how to love like Him.

Chapter Four

Death On The Jerusalem Jericho Highway

"Jesus told her, 'I am the resurrection and the life. Anyone who believes in me will live, even after dying'"

(John 11:25 NLT)

One of the easy to remember and maybe most popular parables of Jesus is the one He shared about the Good Samaritan. Jesus told this story to teach about the subject of love, one to another. A few years ago, I was privileged to have attended the burial of a woman who finished her race well. She was the older sibling of my sister-in-law's husband and had died suddenly. All had seemed well with her the last time I had seen her at a traditional wedding ceremony; it was therefore very shocking to learn of her transition. She was, I believe, in her 50s. One of the striking messages at her funeral was a film depicting graphically how the life of a human is merely a short journey from the womb to the grave. The events that take place between these two points and how we handle them are determinants of the post-resurrection life of every individual.

"Many of those whose bodies lie dead and buried will rise up, some to everlasting life and some to shame and everlasting disgrace"

(Daniel 12:2 NLT)

28

The experience of the Jewish man traveling from Jerusalem to Jericho provides a lesson for every human while on earth. Life is simply a journey from the day we are born to the day our life ends in death. Between these two points, just like in the Samaritan story, man can be attacked by "thieves" whose sole purpose is to steal, kill, and destroy him. They aim to ensure that you do not end your life well–according to God's plan which is for you to gain eternal life. You must, therefore, be wary of the "death" lurking around the corner so that you do not lose your life to sin. "You must be on the alert, stand firm in the faith, act like men and be strong" (1 Corinthians 16:13)

"I am coming soon. Hold on to what you have, so that no one will take away your crown"

(Revelation 3:11 NLT)

Jesus taught us that He expects us to show practical love to others if our purpose is to travel successfully on the journey of life. Those who succeed have been redeemed by the blood of the lamb and are walking in the footsteps of Jesus. Many people have had their lives battered by sin such that they have been left for dead, heading to destruction. The Samaritan example of love, which can be demonstrated by drawing people to Christ, is good for us to emulate. It is Christ alone who can save those under the bondage of sin and turn lives around. A life of fruitlessness, exemplified by the priest and the temple assistant, who both did nothing to help the wounded man, is not a good example for us. The countdown to the return of Jesus has long begun, and many people are "dying in sin" on the Jerusalem-Jericho highway. We must pull all stops and tell it on the mountain that Jesus is coming soon, so all must repent and be born again!

> *"Look! I stand at the door and knock. If you hear my voice and open the door, I will come in, and we will share a meal together as friends"*

(Revelation 3:20 NLT)

Do not "cross to the other side of the road" or abandon the helpless sinners to die in their sins. Show compassion and tell them about Jesus. He alone has the power to deliver and save them. My prayer is that we will all do our best to save ourselves and others from avoidable death on the dangerous highway of life. SHALOM!

Chapter Five

Holiness Tonic

"Then if my people who are called by my name will humble themselves and pray and seek my face and turn from their wicked ways, I will hear from heaven and will forgive their sins and restore their land"

(2 Chronicles 7:14 NLT)

"Godliness makes a nation great, but sin is a disgrace to any people"

(Proverbs 14:34 NLT)

It is usual from time to time that people commit to reflection and planning as they take stock and look to the future. In practice it is good to do so; however since the purpose is to find a way to achieve further progress and success, it would be unwise not to look to God for help, and this help is available ONLY through His word.

"For the wisdom of this world is foolishness to God. As the Scriptures say, 'He traps the wise in the snare of their own cleverness.' And again, 'The Lord knows the thoughts of the wise; He knows they are worthless.'"

(1 Corinthians 3:19–20 NLT)

Many today, after putting on their thinking caps, come up with grand plans on how to address future situations and their challenges. They forget that without the counsel of God and His favor, nothing will go well.

> *"Unless the Lord builds a house, the work of the builders is wasted. Unless the Lord protects a city, guarding it with sentries will do no good"*
>
> *(Psalm 127:1 NLT)*

As you begin each season with your plans and aspirations, do not put God aside. Walk with Him and take His counsel in all that you do…and success is guaranteed.

> *"Trust in the Lord with all your heart; do not depend on your own understanding"*
>
> *(Proverbs 3:5 NLT)*

Remember that God is not fooled. He knows His children, and it is to them alone that He is ready to give His best. Align with God by daily taking a dose of the holiness tonic. To take the holiness tonic means complete obedience to God's word. In this way, your path will be straight. Obey Him in all situations and all ways, and He will honor His covenants and fulfill His promises to you.

> *"Study this book of instruction continually. Meditate on it day and night so you will be sure to obey everything written in it. Only then will you prosper and succeed in all you do"*
>
> *(Joshua 1:8 NLT)*

The Holiness Tonic draws you closer to God as unrepentant sinners cannot be in fellowship with a holy God. The Holiness Tonic is necessary for you to do exploits and do even greater works than Jesus did. The Holiness Tonic allows you to receive classified information from God. The Holiness Tonic builds a wall of protection around you and makes you have peace with your enemies. The Holiness Tonic also helps you to receive divine provision and eternal life. It allows you to remain in God's presence.

If you are not already taking this tonic, start immediately today! Learn to trust God for divine care!

> ***"Cast all your anxiety on Him because He cares for you"***
>
> *(1 Peter 5:7 NLT)*

God bless you.

Chapter Six

If I Must Die, I Must Die

"Go and gather together all the Jews of Susa and fast for me. Do not eat or drink for three days, night or day. My maids and I will do the same. And then, though it is against the law, I will go in to see the king. If I must die, I must die"

(Esther 4:16 NLT)

Jesus never promised those who followed after Him that it would be a bed of roses. If anything, He made it very clear that they would face a tough time and there would be a price to pay if they chose the narrow way to eternal life. The life of an ambassador for Christ is a selfless one focused on continued sacrifice and commitment. Peter reiterated this position, making it clear that suffering is part of the Christian path.

"If you suffer, however, it must not be for murder, stealing, making trouble, or prying into other people's affairs. But it is no shame to suffer for being a Christian. Praise God for the privilege of being called by His name!"

(1 Peter 4:15–16 NLT)

John W. Peterson, in his song titled "It's Not an Easy Road" talked about "thorns" on the way to heaven. This was confirmed by the Babylonian experiences of Daniel and his three Hebrew friends. Notwithstanding, having distinguished themselves in the land of their captivity, they came down for severe persecution because of their commitment to their faith.

"Then they told the king, 'That man Daniel, one of the captives from Judah, is ignoring you and your law. He still prays to his God three times a day'"
(Daniel 6:13 NLT)

The life of John the Baptist was arguably one of the best examples of commitment to a cause. He not only did a perfect job of being the Savior's forerunner but he also "fought a good fight of faith, even to the end" (Matthew 14:1-12). While many would either have chickened out or presented a message that would not get them into trouble, John stood up to be counted and gave his life for the Cross.

"John had been telling Herod, 'It is against God's law for you to marry your brother's wife'"
(Mark 6:18 NLT)

Esther, even as queen, was ready to throw away what would not last for a purpose that was far beyond her and her status. The risk to her life was nothing compared to the goal of saving her people.

As a child of God, this is the example we must follow in our Christian race as exemplified by the Messiah who went to the Cross when He could have called up angels to save Him from His Roman and Jewish persecutors.

> *"No one can take my life from me. I sacrifice it voluntarily. For I have the authority to lay it down when I want to and also to take it up again. For this is what my Father has commanded"*
>
> *(John 10:18 NLT)*

The decision to be committed even unto death, while it may not be easy, comes with the assurance of help from above and a reward for all who complete the race. God cannot be mocked, as whatever we sow, that same thing we will reap. God opened the door to His committed Esther when the king promised to grant her request "even if it is half the Kingdom" (Esther 5:3). He will do likewise for you, provided He is sure of your commitment. Indeed there is a home prepared for you as contained in the words of God and re-echoed in the song "Since I Have Been Redeemed" by Edwin O. Excell.

> *"'Yes," Jesus replied, "and I assure you that everyone who has given up house or brothers or sisters or mother or father or children or property, for my sake and for the Good News, will receive now in return a hundred times as many houses, brothers, sisters, mothers, children, and property— along with persecution. And in the world to come that person will have eternal life"'*
>
> *(Mark 10:29–30 NLT)*

As you reflect on the above message, please take another look at your life to see if you are genuinely committed to your Christian calling. If you are not, I plead with you to be TRULY dedicated to honoring God with your life. God bless you.

Chapter Seven

Jesus Is God's
Lowest Hanging Fruit

God's particular interest in Man as His number one creation is never in doubt. Not only did He make him commander in chief of all His creation, but He also sought to have an intimate relationship with His best by laying down the rule for retaining this friendship right at the beginning. Unfortunately, Man fell at the very first hurdle and lost his perfect relationship with his maker.

> *"But the Lord God warned him, 'You may freely eat the fruit of every tree in the garden—except the tree of the knowledge of good and evil. If you eat its fruit, you are sure to die'"*

> *(Genesis 2:16-17 NLT)*

Although God was disappointed with Man, He nevertheless sought to reestablish this bond by first sieving the wheat from the chaff with the Noah time flood intervention; He did not want to write off man completely. Though this should have been a good chance for man to begin again, he did not take advantage of it. God also sent powerful redemptive messages to the world through His designated prophets so that the world may learn the truth and return to Him.

While some decided to turn back to God, many still wallowed in sin, not willing to reach the level expected from them by the Almighty. For all to be saved, God took another look at the access route to Himself and decided to offer His best package, having seen the shortcomings of the existing offer.

> *"For it is not possible for the blood of bulls and goats to take away sins. That is why, when Christ came into the world, He said to God, 'You did not want animal sacrifices or sin offerings. But you have given me a body to offer. You were not pleased with burnt offerings or other offerings for sin'"*

(Hebrews 10:4-6 NLT)

God presented the "new" salvation package as the lowest hanging fruit possible so that all who come can access it to be free from their sin. Jesus is God's lowest hanging fruit for you. He left His high position and heavenly glory to visit the earth so that He could be made a perfect ransom for all sinners. He made a physical appearance, not only to pay the full price of our redemption but also to show the practical possibility of the life He has called us to live in Him.

Jesus came in complete humility and obedience to His father's plan. His manger birth in the small Jewish town of Bethlehem to a father of lowly status is God's way of showing that no matter your socioeconomic class, Jesus is also accessible to you.

Jesus carved a reputation for Himself as always associating with the spiritually downtrodden. He saw them as the primary purpose for coming into the world and never shied away from them and their needs, no matter the position of the religious leaders. This means that with Him, you too are not lost. There is room available for you at the Cross.

> *"Later, Levi invited Jesus and His disciples to his home as dinner guests, along with many tax collectors and other disreputable sinners. (There were many people of this kind among Jesus' followers.) But when the teachers of religious law, who were Pharisees, saw Him eating with tax collectors and other sinners, they asked his disciples, 'Why does He eat with such scum?' When Jesus heard this, He told them, 'Healthy people don't need a doctor—sick people do. I have come to call not those who think they are righteous, but those who know they are sinners'"*

> *(Mark 2:15–17 NLT)*

Jesus brought a salvation package that is available free of charge. You receive it by grace through faith in God's only begotten son. It has no price tag whatsoever! Unlike in the past, when the rich and poor both struggled in the marketplace for the "best" rams, turtle doves, and young pigeons to buy for sacrifices, this once-in-a-lifetime offering is made the lowest hanging fruit for all and sundry.

God has played His part well. He has made Jesus easily accessible to you. Go to Him right now and confess your sins. Make a firm decision never to go back to your sins again. Jesus will help you and your life will be turned around for good.

> *"However, those the Father has given me will come to me, and I will never reject them"*
>
> *(John 6:37 NLT)*

Chapter Eight

Key To Victory – 1

"The Lord had said to Abram, 'Leave your native country, your relatives, and your father's family, and go to the land that I will show you. I will make you into a great nation. I will bless you and make you famous, and you will be a blessing to others. I will bless those who bless you and curse those who treat you with contempt. All the families on earth will be blessed through you.'"

(Genesis 12:1–3 NLT)

The blessings God promised through Abraham are not a guarantee to all of humanity. I learned long ago that one of the guaranteed ways I can get something from God is to strive always to be in His good books. This I do not claim to have been able to do every time, but one thing that God has shown me very clearly is that the way to His heart and by extension His blessings are ONLY through faith in Christ and obedience to Him. This is the way we can become His friends and gain access to His promises, which are contained in His words.

To reach his lofty height, Abraham paid the price. He had to leave his comfort zone, somewhere he had become so accustomed to and would not want to leave under normal circumstances.

A life desirous of victory requires separation from sin. No matter how used to it or "enjoyable" that life may have become, God is insisting that you have no choice but to let it go and leave it behind forever. You must do exactly as Abraham did.

The new land that God told Abraham to go to is akin to the new life that God is calling you to embrace. He wants you to be a new creature. He wants His light to come into your life. He wants you to put away your flesh and accept His Spirit. There is a clear distinction between the native country of Abraham and the new land God promised to show him. It is ONLY in this new land that he could access God's blessing. It is ONLY in this new life that you too can TRULY be blessed.

You must recognize and appreciate the difference between the life you live now and that which God wants to give you. Just like He promised Abraham a good outcome, He has also promised to go and prepare a place for you. Just like Abraham ultimately became a blessing to all the earth, you too have the opportunity of celebrating in heaven one day.

Abraham went through trials and temptations on the way to his victory. He stumbled along the way but passed the ultimate test on Mount Moriah. You too will face your difficulties. Make sure that whatever it takes, you overcome them, as this is the only way you can be victorious. Determine to end your life in victory; follow the example of Abraham.

I pray that the victory that is available through the resurrection power of Jesus will be yours today. Go and claim your victory!

Chapter Nine

Key To Victory – 2

"Enter His gates with thanksgiving; go into His courts with praise. Give thanks to Him and praise His name. For the Lord is good. His unfailing love continues forever, and His faithfulness continues to each generation"

(Psalm 100: 4–5 NLT)

Some time ago, I was privileged to be at a three-day program at my local church. The guest minister told us the story of a naval officer who was looking forward to being promoted, and because the Bible teaches that promotion does not come from east or west, he decided to seek God's face concerning the matter. On the day he was expecting to be promoted, he was instead served with a retirement letter. He took the letter, went home, and began praising God. His thanksgiving was so remarkable that when his wife returned home, she was curious to know what made her husband so elated. The husband quickly handed her the letter from the military authorities. The wife was shocked to learn that the letter was a retirement notice and wondered why her husband was celebrating. She was worried and concerned for her husband, whom she thought had gone berserk. Against all entreaties, the naval officer went to bed praising God. The next morning, he was visited by four persons who were looking to employ a person with naval experience in a position in the corporate world for which he had been headhunted. Their concern as they sat with him was how to convince him to retire from his commission. The job offered a salary that was almost six times his last military pay. The rest they say is history. He took the offer, as this was the answer to his prayer. He had to be retired before he could accept the job, which was the perfect promotion planned for him. God indeed is faithful!

Some of the other lessons in the program are shared below. Enjoy it!

Jesus taught His disciples that Thanksgiving is a key to victory in two very challenging situations during His lifetime. In both cases, He was faced with seeming human impossibilities, yet He provided solutions to the problems that the people suffered. In both instances, Jesus opened the door of access to His father, who was the remedy source by offering thanks. He merely started by thanking God, making His request and everything He sought came to pass. This is the way for us to follow; our key to victory.

> *"Jesus responded, 'Didn't I tell you that you would see God's glory if you believe?' So they rolled the stone aside. Then Jesus looked up to heaven and said, 'Father, thank You for hearing me. You always hear me, but I said it out loud for the sake of all these people standing here so that they will believe You sent me.' Then Jesus shouted, 'Lazarus,*

come out!' And the dead man came out, his hands and feet bound in grave clothes, his face wrapped in a head cloth. Jesus told them, 'Unwrap him and let him go!'"

(John 11:40–44 NLT)

"Then Jesus took the loaves, gave thanks to God, and distributed them to the people. Afterwards, He did the same with the fish. And they all ate as much as they wanted"

(John 6:11 NLT)

Paul and Silas, too, followed the example of Jesus by offering praise to God at their time of need, and they were not disappointed as they received divine intervention. Though Thanksgiving and praise are not the same thing, both are related and are connected to our efforts at appreciating God. Major battles have been won by simply praising God. Judah's King, Jehoshaphat, overcame three armies using this weapon as his key to victory.

"Then he explained his plan and appointed men to march in front of the army and praise the Lord for his holy power by singing: 'Praise the Lord! His love never ends.' As soon as they began singing, the Lord confused the enemy camp, so that the Ammonite and Moabite troops attacked and completely destroyed those from Edom. Then they turned against each other and fought until the entire camp was wiped out!"

(2 Chronicles 20:21-23 NLT)

God commands that in every situation, we have to give Him thanks. Murmurings are an antithesis to Him. No wonder the servant who got only one talent and complained vehemently had it taken away from him. (Matthew 25:28)

> *"Be thankful in all circumstances, for this is God's will for you who belong to Christ Jesus"*
>
> (I Thessalonians 5:18 NLT)

God deserves our thanks, praise, and worship. They are your keys to His heart and consequently your victory. He is God from the beginning to the end; there is no place for an argument. He is God all by Himself.

Chapter Ten

Lema Sabachthani

"At about three o'clock, Jesus called out with a loud voice, 'Eli, Eli, lema sabachthani?' which means 'My God, my God, why have you abandoned me?'"

(Matthew 27:46 NLT)

Jesus had an extremely close relationship with His father. It is a relationship that many will find very difficult to replicate. He testified to this truth while He was here on earth.

"The Father and I are one"

(John 10:30 NLT)

The closeness between God the father and God the son was such that Jesus told His listeners at the tomb of Lazarus that His father always hears Him.

"So they rolled the stone aside. Then Jesus looked up to heaven and said, 'Father, thank You for hearing me. You always hear me, but I said it out loud for the sake of all these people standing here so that they will believe You sent me'"

(John 11:41–42 NLT)

What then could have happened at the Cross? Since Jesus could not have made a wrong assertion, then we can say with all assurance that indeed His father forsook Him at that very point. What was the new status of Jesus that made this rejection to happen? Jesus' sole purpose of visiting the earth was to carry out God's redemptive plan of Salvation. In order to achieve this, He needed to offer himself as a ransom for the sin of all men. This way, He took away our sins and died in our place.

> *"The next day John saw Jesus coming toward him and said, 'Look! The Lamb of God who takes away the sin of the world!'"*
>
> *(John 1:29 NLT)*

> *"He personally carried our sins in His body on the Cross so that we can be dead to sin and live for what is right"*
>
> *(1 Peter 2:24a NLT)*

The rejection that Jesus experienced was as a result of His carrying the sin of the whole of humanity upon Himself. God hates sin though He loves the sinner. He is uncompromising in His hatred for sin; He adopts a permanent position of sin rejection no matter who the sinner is or who is carrying the sin as in the case of Jesus. Nothing can make Him change this position since He did not change it even in the case of Jesus.

> *"There are six things the Lord hates—no, seven things He detests: haughty eyes, a lying tongue, hands that kill the innocent, a heart that plots evil, feet that race to do*

wrong, a false witness who pours out lies, a person who sows discord in a family"

(Proverbs 6:16–19 NLT)

Joseph was an example of a man who lived a life in the knowledge of God's hatred for sin, and so notwithstanding the considerable incentive he had from the mother of the house, he rejected sin and so triumphed over a situation that could have truncated his destiny.

"No one here has more authority than I do. He has held back nothing from me except you because you are his wife. How could I do such a wicked thing? It would be a great sin against God"

(Genesis 39:9 NLT)

Reuben, on the other hand, went for the transient allure of sin pleasure and in doing so lost his inheritance. As firstborn, he had a higher potential to excel than Joseph, but he threw it away on a platter of sin. I am sure that he would have bitterly wept when his father pronounced his final testament, but there was nothing he could do about it again.

"'Reuben, you are my firstborn, my strength, the child of my vigorous youth. You are first in rank and first in power. But you are as unruly as a flood, and you will be first no longer. For you went to bed with my wife; you defiled my marriage couch'"

(Genesis 49:3-4 NLT)

Saul and David both suffered different consequences of sin. One thing that is clear from their life stories is that NOTHING IS HIDDEN FROM GOD. We may indeed cover our sins that no one else will know, BUT WE CAN NEVER HIDE IT FROM GOD. They must, as kings, have limitless resources that could hide sin from man BUT NEITHER COULD HIDE IT FROM GOD.

> *"I am watching them closely, and I see every sin. They cannot hope to hide from me"*
>
> *(Jeremiah 16:17 NLT)*

Dearly beloved, God in temporarily forsaking Jesus proved to us that He does not compromise His standards when it comes to the rejection of sin and neither does He apply favoritism. Sin has remained the ONLY "barrier" building a gulf and creating enmity between man and God. For anyone intending to have a profitable relationship with God, total sin rejection is a must.

> *"Listen! The Lord's arm is not too weak to save you, nor is His ear too deaf to hear you call. It's your sins that have cut you off from God. Because of your sins, He has turned away and will not listen anymore. Your hands are the hands of murderers, and your fingers are filthy with sin. Your lips are full of lies, and your mouth spews corruption"*
>
> *(Isaiah 59: 1–3 NLT)*

This is God's position on sin, and it is UNCHANGEABLE. As you reflect on these words, I implore you to search your life and examine if there is any sin that will make God not see eye-to-eye with you. Do away with it because YOU CANNOT HIDE IT FROM GOD.

God bless you.

Chapter Eleven

Ojo Nla Ni Ojo Na

"Mark my words—I will not drink wine again until the day I drink it new with you in my Father's Kingdom"

(Matthew 26:29 NLT)

Jesus spoke the above words at the end of the last meal He had with His disciples. The whole essence of His coming into the world was to prepare us for that particular day so that we can join Him to drink the wine again. He told His disciples more than 40 parables just because He wants them and all who hear His words to experience great joy on that day. He allowed Himself to be bruised and ultimately taken to the Cross because that is the only way we can receive the redemption that will qualify us to attend the marriage supper of the Lamb. OJO NLA NI OJO NA in the Yoruba language means GREAT IS THAT DAY!

On Easter Monday, I attended a baptismal service followed by the observation of the Lord's Supper in my church. It was a compelling service full of sober and deep reflection. One of the familiar songs of the day talked about the day of our salvation being a great day. It warned of the need to be very prayerful as we start our walk in the Lord Jesus Christ. It counseled that we must be careful so as not to miss our way. It encourages us to be joyful as light has finally come into our life. A great day indeed; the day Jesus washed away our sins.

God hates sin with a passion, and this disgust is illustrated in the book of Hosea by the Prophet when God asked him to marry a prostitute. Our body is the temple of God and, having been created in His image, He expects profound intimacy with us as His friends. Unfortunately, many of us care so little about this and so go ahead to use our body any way we want, not minding the grief it brings to our creator.

Another great day is coming; maybe even more significant than the first. This day will be a terrible day. It is a day where everything will be revealed, and nothing will be hidden any longer. It will be a day of unparalleled anguish and also one of great joy. Many will dread to see that day but will be inevitable to miss out on it. A confident, rich man experienced the anguish of that great day and wished he could reverse it while Lazarus experienced the joy of that day and realized all his pains and suffering on earth was worth every bit of it.

> *"The rich man shouted, 'Father Abraham, have some pity! Send Lazarus over here to dip the tip of his finger in water and cool my tongue. I am in anguish in these flames'"*
>
> *(Luke 16:24 NLT)*

Beloved, you cannot afford to take with levity the issue of this great day. The offer of salvation to you must not be taken for granted. Many are daily being born, and many more are dying. Take advantage of what is offered to you by the Nazarene and do not delay any further. He desires to see your face at the heavenly supper. Proceed to embrace a life of holiness as you prepare for this great day. Remember God is not mocked. You will reap whatever you sow.

I pray that you will not be found wanting on that great day in Jesus' name. Amen.

Chapter Twelve

Remember The Cross

"God saved you by His grace when you believed. And you can't take credit for this; it is a gift from God. Salvation is not a reward for the good things we have done, so none of us can boast about it"

(Ephesians 2: 8 – 9 NLT)

I saw the caption "Remember the Cross" on the back of a commercial bus driving ahead of me on the Lagos Ibadan Expressway, and I have never forgotten it. The more I reflect on it, the more I gain profound insights into all that the Cross entails. The caption spoke volumes to me. It is somewhat like a warning, though the Cross is about sacrificial love. The Cross refers to the story of a man who acted unusually…all for the sake of love.

"There is no greater love than to lay down one's life for one's friends"

(John 15:13 NLT)

Jesus' action on the Golgotha way up to the Cross was unprecedented. No one is ever known to have offered his life in exchange for a guilty man. He had many opportunities to extricate Himself from shameful death starting from the trial at Pilate's court where He even had an advocate in

His judge's wife. He chose to confound all and go ahead to complete His assignment with perfection on the Cross.

> *"When Jesus had tasted it, He said, 'It is finished!' Then He bowed His head and gave up His spirit"*

> *(John 19:30 NLT)*

The work that Jesus completed on the Cross is to address the inadequacy of the never-ending use of the blood of animals as an atonement for sin. Jesus came to put finality on the salvation plan of God making all other options a nullity. The salvation offered by Jesus is accessible to anyone who accepts Him by faith. It cannot be attained by our perceived good works, which are as filthy rags in the sight of God.

> *"The old system under the law of Moses was only a shadow, a dim preview of the good things to come, not the good things themselves. The sacrifices under that system were repeated again and again, year after year, but they were never able to provide perfect cleansing for those who came to worship. If they could have provided perfect cleansing, the sacrifices would have stopped, for the worshipers would have been purified once for all time, and their feelings of guilt would have disappeared. But instead, those sacrifices actually reminded them of their sins year after year. For it is not possible for the blood of bulls and goats to take away sins"*

> *(Hebrews 10:1–4 NLT)*

> *First, Christ said, "You did not want animal sacrifices or sin offerings or burnt offerings or other offerings for sin, nor were You pleased with them" (though they are required by the law of Moses). Then He said, "Look, I have come to do Your will." He cancels the first covenant in order to put the second into effect. For God's will was for us to be made holy by the sacrifice of the body of Jesus Christ, once for all time*

> *(Hebrews 10: 8 – 10 NLT)*

The message of the Cross comes with consequences and something about the caption on the bus smacks of the need to send out a warning to all. Jesus did confirm the existence of this consequence while He was on the Cross. He was crucified between two thieves, both having been rightly found guilty of their crimes. While one made a passionate plea to Jesus for mercy, the other, not feeling any remorse for his sins, scorned him. Each of them ended with different outcomes.

> *"One of the criminals hanging beside Him scoffed, 'So you're the Messiah, are you? Prove it by saving Yourself—and us, too, while you're at it!' But the other criminal protested, 'Don't you fear God even when you have been sentenced to die? We deserve to die for our crimes, but this man hasn't done anything wrong.' Then he said, 'Jesus, remember me when You come into Your Kingdom.' And Jesus replied, 'I assure you, today you will be with me in paradise'"*

> *(Luke 23:39–43 NLT)*

To remember the Cross means we must take advantage of Jesus' offer to save us. The existence of the Cross brings to mind the truth that if we do not accept this offer, there will be irreversible, painful, and regrettable consequences. The free salvation package of Jesus completed on the Cross is AGAIN being offered to you today. The best action to take is to confess your sins, ask for mercy, and surrender your life entirely to Jesus. As you remember the Cross today, do not allow the price Jesus paid for you to become wasted. I pray that you will respond positively to this offer and find a place in your heart for Jesus. JESUS IS COMING AGAIN VERY SOON! REMEMBER THE CROSS.

Chapter Thirteen

The Good Shepherd

"The thief's purpose is to steal and kill and destroy. My purpose is to give them a rich and satisfying life"

(John 10:10 NLT)

Jesus in defining His role brought to the fore the fact that man is continuously exposed to the risk of deceit. In referring to Himself as the good shepherd, He was from all practical purposes saying that there is a bad shepherd somewhere someplace who we must avoid at all cost. He did an excellent job of differentiating Himself from the other shepherd in the manner of approach to the flock. He talked about voice identification, His unwavering commitment, and the ultimate sacrifice He made for the sheep which sets Him apart from the evil shepherd. He calls this other shepherd a thief.

"I am the good shepherd. The good shepherd sacrifices his life for the sheep. A hired hand will run when he sees a wolf coming. He will abandon the sheep because they don't belong to him and he isn't their shepherd. And so the wolf attacks them and scatters the flock. The hired hand runs away because he's working only for the money and doesn't really care about the sheep"

(John10:11–13 NLT)

Jesus called the other shepherd "a thief" because of the dire consequences to which he puts those who allow him to lead them. He summarised these consequences as steal, kill, and destroy. The word "thief" here refers to false teachers who are motivated to mislead the world by their evil master: the Devil. Jesus warns that those who reject the comfort and peace He offers for the false promise of the thief will pay dearly for it.

This thief will steal your salvation if you allow him.

> *"I am coming soon. Hold on to what you have, so that no one will take away your crown"*

> *(Revelation 3:11 NLT)*

This thief will kill you spiritually if you let him.

> *"Stay alert! Watch out for your great enemy, the devil. He prowls around like a roaring lion, looking for someone to devour"*

> *(1 Peter 5:8 NLT)*

This thief will finally destroy you at the end of the age if you don't turn to Jesus now. He is heading for destruction and wants to take you along. Would you allow him?

> *"Then the devil, who had deceived them, was thrown into the fiery lake of burning sulfur, joining the beast and the false prophet. There they will be tormented day and night forever and ever"*

> *(Revelation 20:10 NLT)*

There is a choice for you to make between the good shepherd and the thief. You cannot sit on the fence. Jesus is prepared to shepherd you to God's eternal kingdom. Why not give him a chance?

> *"Yes, I am the gate. Those who come in through me will be saved. They will come and go freely and will find good pastures"*
>
> *(John 10:9 NLT)*

I pray that you will follow after the good shepherd and enjoy His pasture.

Chapter Fourteen

The Road To Golgotha

The road to Golgotha started in a little town called Bethlehem and ended at the "place of the skull" where Jesus finished the salvation work of God by giving up His life for all. Indeed "it is finished" as the baby born to Mary and Joseph completed God's redemption plan for humanity. The Golgotha "highway," though leading to the beautiful city of God, was paved not with gold but with the blood of the Savior. Jesus willingly offered Himself for crucifixion to give all who care to come access to the holy city: Jerusalem.

> *"The wall was made of Jasper, and the city was pure gold, as clear as glass. The wall of the city was built on foundation stones inlaid with twelve precious stones: the first was jasper, the second sapphire, the third agate, the fourth emerald, the fifth onyx, the sixth carnelian, the seventh chrysolite, the eighth beryl, the ninth topaz, the tenth chrysoprase, the eleventh jacinth, the twelfth amethyst. The twelve gates were made of pearls—each gate from a single pearl! And the main street was pure gold, as clear as glass"*

(Revelation 21:18–21 NLT)

The Golgotha plan was put together by God because of the inadequacy of the blood of animals. God saw that man was heading for permanent destruction if something drastic and special was not done to save him. He, therefore, arranged a once-and-for-all package that was good enough for His creation. Jesus agreed to this plan by abandoning His divine privileges to come down to earth in human form.

> *"You must have the same attitude that Christ Jesus had. Though He was God, He did not think of equality with God as something to cling to. Instead, He gave up His divine privileges; He took the humble position of a slave and was born as a human being. When He appeared in human form, He humbled Himself in obedience to God and died a criminal's death on a cross"*

(Philippians 2:5–8 NLT)

Jesus has set for you the Golgotha example of sacrifice, self-denial, and focus. It is an example that all who seek to follow after Him must emulate. Though it does not come cheap, it is possible to achieve and sure to be rewarded.

> *"Then Jesus said to His disciples, 'If any of you wants to be my follower, you must give up your own way, take up your cross, and follow me. If you try to hang on to your life, you will lose it. But if you give up your life for my sake, you will save it. And what do you benefit if you gain the whole world but lose your own soul? Is anything worth more than your soul?"*

(Matthew 16:24–26 NLT)

65

Jesus faced a lot of temptations on His way to Calvary, and the same must come to all His friends. To overcome, the way to go is to follow the example of Christ. Jesus defeated His enemies with the Word of God which is sharper than a two-edged sword. You too have access to the Word and must never fail to apply the same at all times. He went through His Golgotha experience to save you from eternal condemnation. Though driven by love, Jesus is unable to do more than die for you. His salvation package is enough for you, but you must take the necessary step of turning away from your sins and embracing this offer. Anything else will be foolhardy and disastrous.

"I saw no temple in the city, for the Lord God Almighty and the Lamb are its temple. And the city has no need of sun or moon, for the glory of God illuminates the city, and the Lamb is its light. The nations will walk in its light, and the kings of the world will enter the city in all their glory. Its gates will never be closed at the end of day because there is no night there. And all the nations will bring their glory and honor into the city. Nothing evil will be allowed to enter, nor anyone who practices shameful idolatry and dishonesty—but only those whose names are written in the Lamb's Book of Life"

(Revelation 21:22–27 NLT)

Have you given your life to Jesus? Has your name been written in the Book of Life? Take time to remember His

Golgotha experience and reconcile yourself to the Savior of humanity. Jesus loves you, and He is coming again!

God bless you!

Chapter Fifteen

The Savior Of All Mankind

"But the angel reassured them. 'Don't be afraid!' he said. 'I bring you good news that will bring great joy to all people. The Savior—yes, the Messiah, the Lord— has been born today in Bethlehem, the city of David!'"

(Luke 2:10–11 NLT)

The Salvation that Jesus offers you is both physical and spiritual. You only need to go to Him, and He will never cast you away. His Salvation gift is also for all; no one is excluded provided they come in faith with an open and sincere heart. No one can save you from your situation except Jesus the Christ.

"A woman in the crowd had suffered for twelve years with constant bleeding, and she could find no cure. Coming up behind Jesus, she touched the fringe of His robe. Immediately, the bleeding stopped"

(Luke 8:43–44 NLT)

The purpose of Jesus coming is to save humanity from sin and death. Man came into the world carrying the Adamic baggage of sin. He cannot help himself even when he has a deep-seated hatred and dislike for sin. Many find themselves wallowing in sin without the ability to let go of it. Only Jesus can deliver the sinner.

> *"For I was born a sinner—yes, from the moment my mother conceived me"*
>
> *(Psalm 51:5 NLT)*

The Salvation package that Jesus offers is one in which our justification is made possible only by our faith in Him. There is nothing else to the matter. Nothing we can do for ourselves will be adequate. Our righteousness cannot measure up to the standard set by God.

> *"Yet we know that a person is made right with God by faith in Jesus Christ, not by obeying the law. And we have believed in Christ Jesus so that we might be made right with God because of our faith in Christ, not because we have obeyed the law. For no one will ever be made right with God by obeying the law"*
>
> *(Galatians 2:16 NLT)*

This Salvation is unmerited. It is made possible by grace. It has nothing to do with what you have done or can do. Jesus was offered free to pay the full price of your redemption and reconciliation back to God.

> *"God saved you by His grace when you believed. And you can't take credit for this; it is a gift from God. Salvation is not a reward for the good things we have done, so none of us can boast about it"*
>
> *(Ephesians 2:8–9 NLT)*

The Salvation made available to you in Christ Jesus needs to be guarded jealously. It is not meat and drink, and neither is it an end in itself. You have it within you to make a success of your Salvation opportunity. However, you may lose it and become worse off than you were before accepting Christ if you do not take heed.

> *"For it is impossible to bring back to repentance those who were once enlightened —those who have experienced the good things of heaven and shared in the Holy Spirit, who have tasted the goodness of the word of God and the power of the age to come—and who then turn away from God. It is impossible to bring such people back to repentance; by rejecting the Son of God, they themselves are nailing him to the Cross once again and holding him up to public shame"*
>
> *(Hebrews 6:4–6 NLT)*

The Savior of all humanity came so that you will have life and have it more abundantly. Jesus came to give you a chance to gain access to eternal life, but that is it. He cannot travel on the narrow way for you. You must walk the walk yourself through a life of holiness if you are intent on gaining entry into His father's kingdom. The Savior of humanity will return one day as the judge of the whole universe and everything will be laid bare at His feet. As you celebrate the dawn of another day, do an audit of your life and take necessary action to align your life with Jesus' expectations.

Chapter Sixteen

Two Lessons For The Same Prize

"'For I was hungry, and you fed me. I was thirsty, and you gave me a drink. I was a stranger, and you invited me into your home. I was naked, and you gave me clothing. I was sick, and you cared for me. I was in prison, and you visited me.' Then these righteous ones will reply, 'Lord, when did we ever see You hungry and feed you? Or thirsty and give you something to drink? Or a stranger and show you hospitality? Or naked and give you clothing? When did we ever see you sick or in prison and visit you?' And the King will say, 'I tell you the truth when you did it to one of the least of these my brothers and sisters, you were doing it to me!'"

(Matthew 25:35–40 NLT)

"But cowards, unbelievers, the corrupt, murderers, the immoral, those who practice witchcraft, idol worshipers, and all liars— their fate is in the fiery lake of burning sulfur. This is the second death"

(Revelation 21:8 NLT)

"Nothing evil will be allowed to enter, nor anyone who practices shameful idolatry and dishonesty—but only those whose names are written in the Lamb's Book of Life"

(Revelation 21:17 NLT)

The fact that life is a continuum means that we should be interested and also concerned about what will happen to us after our mortal bodies stop functioning. The reality is that one day, our life will come to an end. It is, as they say, one debt that all peoples of the world owe and must pay one day or the other. The Bible provides clear insight into man's fate once he closes his eyes in death.

> *"And just as each person is destined to die once and after that comes judgment"*
>
> *(Hebrews 9:27 NLT)*

This judgment is a transition phase that is followed by life in eternity. The other reality is that life in eternity can either be in commendation or condemnation. This is the very reason why Jesus came to the world; He came to help us come to the saving knowledge of God, and so avoid life in eternal condemnation. To avoid this terrible experience, it is good we remind ourselves of the expectations of the judge, whom we will stand before when we finally close our eyes.

One of the misconceptions of today is that which relegates the importance of our faith in Christ combined with holiness but puts forward good works as being enough to grant us passage to eternal life. This is a fallacy of the highest proportion and does not agree with the message of Jesus on the final judgment (Matthew 25: 31 – 46).

Many people see their "good works" and a show of kindness as all they need to please God and meet His commendation criteria. What a pity! Many will face a regret that cannot be reversed. Though it is good to show kindness and indeed it is one of the fruits of the spirit, however, the foundation is important, and there is no other foundation than that which is built on Christ Jesus. This is the first and most important step before we can qualify for commendation.

Many wicked people hide under assumed "protection" in God's house by being actively involved in one form of giving or the other. Unfortunately, all these will be tested and ultimately burnt and be of no value at the judgment throne. In the parable of Jesus, He had already identified some as sheep, which is a symbolic sign of obedience and humility. It is the sheep that bore the fruit of kindness which Jesus referred to in the story. It is these sheep that are also called the righteous in the passage. To be righteous means to be morally correct or justifiable, so it is not only enough that you show kindness and help your neighbor. Do not be fooled, as feeding your whole village or building the biggest cathedral will not sway God to embrace a life filled with sin. Even this He did not do to His son when He was carrying the sins of the whole world on the Cross. He will not bend the rules for you, sir! He hates sin with a passion!

Dearly beloved, a life of kindness without holiness means nothing to God. This is why He gave that clear position to Apostle John in His revelation to him. If you like, buy a car for your pastor or train all the indigent students in your village; but if you don't forsake your sins, God will reject you on the last day. You have been warned! Nothing evil will find its way to the new city! For those who are already in Christ, we are encouraged to bear fruits of kindness and to show love. In this way, our faith will be said to have good works.

A life of religiosity without foundation in Christ is commonplace in the world. It is not a life that pleases God and so it will be cast away just like the "goats" on the last day. Take a stand for the truth and let your life reflect this truth till the end. The lessons of kindness and holiness are two, but the prize is the same. I pray that when the roll is called up yonder, you and I will be there!

Chapter Seventeen

Watch And Pray

"How you are fallen from heaven, O shining star, son of the morning! You have been thrown down to the earth, you who destroyed the nations of the world. For you said to yourself, 'I will ascend to heaven and set my throne above God's stars. I will preside on the mountain of the gods far away in the north. I will climb to the highest heavens and be like the Most High.' Instead, you will be brought down to the place of the dead, down to its lowest depths"

(Isaiah 14:12–15 NLT)

The chief architect of temptation has been active since he was cast down by God Almighty. He has been extremely busy and tireless in his search for those who will join him in eternal condemnation and destruction. Even the son of God was not spared from the efforts of the NUMBER ONE ACCUSER OF MEN.

Jesus appreciated the risk and potential consequences of falling into temptation, and He advised His followers to watch and pray.

"Keep watch and pray, so that you will not give in to temptation. For the spirit is willing, but the body is weak!"

(Matthew 26:41 NLT)

Peter was one of the most self-assured disciples of Jesus. He was warned of coming temptation and was privileged to be among those who heard the watch and pray admonition directly from Jesus. Yet, when the wily and crafty deceiver came to him on a cold night in Jerusalem, it took just the efforts of two servant girls and a bystander for him to be knocked out cold. He gave in to the fear of personal safety.

God testified concerning David that he was a man after His own heart. He even boasted that "he will do everything I want him to do" (Acts 13:12), yet when he was "visited" by the "father of lies" who came to him at the balcony of his royal palace late one afternoon when he was supposed to be at war like most kings, David disappointed himself and God by giving in to temptation. He saw the wife of one of his soldiers and could not get her off his mind. He not only committed the sin of adultery with her, but he also went on to arrange the death of her husband to cover up his crime. He forgot that God is omniscient and omnipresent. It was a double-headed fall driven by a desire for the opposite sex.

Elisha had the privilege of serving under Elijah, and at the exit of his spiritual father, he received a double portion of his anointing. Gehazi took the position of assistant to Elisha and must have learned from his master all that was expected from a prophet's understudy. He will also have seen first-hand the power of God being manifested in Elisha's life as a true prophet of God through the many miracles being performed by him. Though he was taught by Elisha that "freely you have received and freely you must give" yet the "thief" came to tempt him by encouraging the use of his master's name to extort money from Naaman falsely. He faced an unprecedented consequence for his action driven by the love of money.

King Saul also faced the temptation of the wicked one, but in his case, it was the fear of the people that brought him to his knees, leaving the devil smiling away in victory.

> *"Then Saul admitted to Samuel, 'Yes, I have sinned. I have disobeyed your instructions and the Lord's command, for I was afraid of the people and did what they demanded'"*

(1 Samuel 15:24 NLT)

All these men—Peter, David, Gehazi, and Saul—were either anointed or connected to the source of supernatural power. Nevertheless, they came under the temptation threat of the ruler of this world, and they all fell YAKATAYAGWA (translated as completely) to the ground from their high horses. You, too, are not insulated from temptation. Falling into temptation will lead you away from eternal life. Watch and pray so as to live a victorious life.

My prayer is that you will always escape the tempter's snare in Jesus' name. Amen.

Chapter Eighteen

Zion's King On A Cross

"Therefore Pilate said to Him, 'So, you are a king?' Jesus answered, 'You say correctly that I am a king. For this, I have been born, and for this I have come into the world, to testify to the truth. Everyone who is of the truth hears My voice'"

(John 18:37 NASB)

The status of Jesus as a king is not in doubt. He made this very clear when speaking to Pilate. What is unique about this particular King was His willingness to leave His kingdom and come to the earth to end up on a cross. There were many other things unusual about this King. Unlike most earthly kings of His time, He walked on foot most of the time, and when He had to ride an animal, He chose a donkey, not a horse, a chariot, or a carriage. He is a humble peace-loving king. He indeed is our peace.

"And since I, your Lord and Teacher, have washed your feet, you ought to wash each other's feet. I have given you an example to follow. Do as I have done to you"

(John 13:14, 15 NLT)

This King never engaged in frivolities. Unlike most earthly kings, who see themselves as gods to be served, Jesus focused on His father's assignment and was unwavering to see it to a successful end. This King demonstrated unrivaled love and did not hold back anything from His friends. Unlike earthly kings, who under normal circumstances will be the last to die, Jesus willingly offered Himself as a ransom for the whole world.

> *"No one can take my life from me. I sacrifice it voluntarily. For I have the authority to lay it down when I want to and also to take it up again. For this is what my Father has commanded"*
>
> *(John 10:18 NLT)*

This King abandoned all His royal paraphernalia just for you. He accepted the worst kind of death to pay the full price for your redemption. Nothing could make Him turn back because the hope of humanity would have been dashed.

> *"Instead, He gave up His divine privileges, and he took the humble position of a slave by being born as a human being. When He appeared in human form, He humbled Himself in obedience to God and died a criminal's death on a cross"*
>
> *(Philippians 2:7-8 NLT)*

So why did this king accept to die on a cross? Jesus wants you to have, through His death, a visa to enter His kingdom. A place in His kingdom is reserved for all who believe in Jesus and live their lives modeled after His own.

Take advantage of the sacrifice He made on the Cross. Do not allow His death and resurrection to be a waste. Get a visa to meet the king. Give your life to Christ!

Chapter Nineteen

Jesus Is Coming Today Or Tomorrow

"Look, I am coming soon, bringing my reward with me to repay all people according to their deeds"

(Revelation 22:12 NLT)

A story was told at a Christian gathering in which I was lucky to be in attendance. One of the ministers there shared a vision that God gave to him. In the vision, God told him that only ten persons in his hometown were found worthy of eternal life on that particular day.

Although one could argue whether the ten persons in the vision are real or symbolic, the truth is that God was warning the people that only a few of them were on the narrow way to eternal life. Another reality is that this figure may be representative of the larger country of Nigeria—or the world—and this should concern you. The question to ask is whether you, as a reader, or myself, as a writer, belong to this very minute number.

You may be one of the highly focused, hardworking, diligent and result-oriented persons in your community. You may have immensely enjoyed God's unmerited favor and unwavering faithfulness. Again, by all standards, one could say that you have achieved a good measure of success and done well for yourself. God may have also blessed you financially. In every possible way, your life may be looking up. However, today I wish that you would turn your attention in another direction...a direction that focuses on walking in the way of the Lord and always watching and waiting for His return.

The famous songwriter, Fanny Crosby, received inspiration to channel our thoughts toward the same direction; the time Jesus will come back to reward His servants. She asserted in one of her songs that those whom the Lord will find watching are blessed and that THEY WILL SHARE IN HIS GLORY.

In the parable of the rich man and Lazarus, Jesus taught us a very important lesson on regret. The rich man in question had lived his life without regard for God, and when he died, he found himself in hell. Though he could not turn back the hand of the clock, he knew the importance of reaching out to his family so that they could avoid the calamity that had befallen him in hellfire.

> *"Then the rich man said, 'Please, Father Abraham, at least send him to my father's home. For I have five brothers, and I want him to warn them, so they don't end up in this place of torment'"*
>
> *(Luke 16:27 NLT)*

For God says, "At just the right time, I heard you. On the day of salvation, I helped you." Indeed, the "right time" is now. Today is the day of salvation.

(2 Corinthians 6:2 NLT)

All humans are different from each other—each with their calling and vocation. It will, therefore, be impossible for us to behave and act alike. Even identical twin siblings are known to have their differences. The diversity in our lifestyles must not sway us from the requirement of God for all to believe in Jesus and obey His commandments. This is not anyone's charge but the word of God which is non-negotiable.

"Nothing evil will be allowed to enter, nor anyone who practices shameful idolatry and dishonesty—but only those whose names are written in the Lamb's Book of Life"

(Revelation 21:27 NLT)

All of us are on a journey. We were born one day, and we will surely leave the world someday. We, of course, love life and want to live for a long time, but the reality is that anyone born of a woman must die. This is a debt that we all owe. Since we all must die, then it is essential that we think about what will happen after we die.

"And just as each person is destined to die once and after that comes judgment"

(Hebrews 9:27 NLT)

I know we all have different backgrounds and persuasions. This notwithstanding, we must understand that the word of God is settled in heaven. This means that no matter how much lip service we pay to the Bible and how much we relegate it to the background, it is the mind of God and it tells us about Him and how He will rule over His creation.

> *"Heaven and earth will disappear, but my words will never disappear"*

> *(Matthew 24:35 NLT)*

For a moment, please think of yourself as a part of a herd of cattle. The purpose of a shepherd is to protect his flock from all danger and lead them to a place of good pasture. Today, I see the same scenario playing out in our lives. Jesus is the good shepherd, and His sole purpose is to keep us to Himself and protect us from all evil—and after that lead us to eternal life if we allow Him. My charge to us is to see to it that we do not just succeed in this world but that we find a way to enjoy continued success by finding entry into God's eternal kingdom. For me, success means that when the roll is called up yonder, my name is found in the Book of Life.

> *"And anyone whose name was not found recorded in the Book of Life was thrown into the lake of fire"*

> *(Revelation 20:15 NLT)*

Time flies so quickly, and whether we like it or not, we will one day be ready to go into our grave. To think about death is wise and good, for we must prepare for it. To prepare for it is to put our house in order with God. We can enjoy many things in this world, but one day, all will come to an end. We will be powerless to stop death. On that day, money, wine, and women or men will mean nothing. Houses, clothes, and cars will be useless to us. Even family members cannot come to our aid any longer. We will be all by ourselves, left alone to face God and the consequences of our living. Those who say they love us will only watch from afar. It is a day that must never meet us unprepared.

> *"A wise person thinks a lot about death, while a fool thinks only about having a good time"*
>
> *(Ecclesiastes 7:4 NLT)*

> *"Remember Him before you become fearful of falling and worry about danger in the streets; before your hair turns white like an almond tree in bloom, and you drag along without energy like a dying grasshopper, and the caperberry no longer inspires sexual desire. Remember Him before you near the grave, your everlasting home, when the mourners will weep at your funeral. Yes, remember your Creator now while you are young, before the silver cord of life snaps and the golden bowl is broken. Don't wait until the water jar is smashed at the spring and the pulley is broken at the well. For then the dust will return to the earth, and the spirit will return to God who gave it"*

> *(Ecclesiastes 12:5–7 NLT)*

Jesus is coming today or tomorrow means that before long, I who write this message must face God's judgment throne. All of us will. The things of this world are in the hands of the ruler of this world to use in turning the minds of men away from God. The fact that we know this means we are one step away from defeating him. Though the battle is fierce, we must fight the good fight of faith until we receive our crown. To lose the battle for our soul is not an option.

> *"And this world is fading away, along with everything that people crave. But anyone who does what pleases God will live forever"*

> *(1 John 2:17 NLT)*

> *"And what do you benefit if you gain the whole world but lose your own soul?"*

> *(Mark 8:36 NLT)*

I plead with you to reflect on these few words and take necessary action.

May the Lord bless and protect you. May the Lord smile on you and be gracious to you. May the Lord show you His favor and give you His peace. Amen in Jesus' name.

Chapter Twenty

Prophet, Priest And King

"Long ago God spoke many times and in many ways to our ancestors through the prophets. And now in these final days, He has spoken to us through His Son. God promised everything to the Son as an inheritance, and through the Son, He created the universe. The Son radiates God's own glory and expresses the very character of God, and He sustains everything by the mighty power of His command. When He had cleansed us from our sins, He sat down in the place of honor at the right hand of the majestic God in heaven"

(Hebrews 1:1–3 NLT)

A wedding ceremony is a significant and solemn occasion, as the union being created is similar to that which exists between Christ and the Church. I had the privilege of attending a wedding ceremony some time ago, and while I will be quick to give kudos to the families for putting together an excellent event, my biggest take away was in one of the songs used for the program: Fanny Crosby's very popular hymn "Praise Him! Praise Him!" Though not a new song to me, Crosby's reference to Jesus as Prophet, Priest, and King remained with me long after the end of the marriage ceremony.

Jesus as Prophet

Jesus told His disciples many things about the future, and they all came to pass.

> *"I have told you these things so that you won't abandon your faith. For you will be expelled from the synagogues, and the time is coming when those who kill you will think they are doing a holy service for God"*

> *(John 16: 1–2 NLT)*

> *"As Jesus was going up to Jerusalem, He took the twelve disciples aside privately and told them what was going to happen to Him. 'Listen,' He said, "we're going up to Jerusalem, where the Son of Man will be betrayed to the leading priests and the teachers of religious law. They will sentence Him to die. Then they will hand Him over to the Romans to be mocked, flogged with a whip, and crucified. But on the third day, He will be raised from the dead"'*

> *(Matthew 20: 17–19 NLT)*

Jesus as Priest

Jesus perfectly played the intercessory role between man and God.

> *"But our High Priest offered himself to God as a single sacrifice for sins, good for all time. Then He sat down in the place of*

honor at God's right hand. There He waits until His enemies are humbled and made a footstool under His feet. For by that one offering He forever made perfect those who are being made holy"

(Hebrews 10:12–14 NLT)

"So Christ has now become the High Priest over all the good things that have come. He has entered that greater, more perfect Tabernacle in heaven, which was not made by human hands and is not part of this created world. With His own blood—not the blood of goats and calves—He entered the Most Holy Place once for all time and secured our redemption forever"

(Hebrews 9:11–12 NLT)

"In this way, God qualified Him as a perfect High Priest, and He became the source of eternal salvation for all those who obey Him. And God designated Him to be a High Priest in the order of Melchizedek"

(Hebrews 5:9–10 NLT)

Jesus as King

Jesus testified to His royal status as king.

"Jesus answered, 'My Kingdom is not an earthly kingdom. If it were, my followers would fight to keep me from being handed

over to the Jewish leaders. But my Kingdom is not of this world.' Pilate said, 'So you are a king?' Jesus responded, 'You say I am a king. Actually, I was born and came into the world to testify to the truth. All who love the truth recognize that what I say is true'"

(John 18:36–37 NLT)

This King is coming again, and His reward is with Him. Jesus Christ indeed is Prophet, Priest, and King. The uniqueness is that He is the Son, not a mere prophet; He is the final sacrifice, the Priest, and the Temple; and He is not just Israel's greatest King, but the King of all creation! Are you ready for the return of Jesus Christ the King?

"Then I saw heaven opened, and a white horse was standing there. Its rider was named Faithful and True, for he judges fairly and wages a righteous war. His eyes were like flames of fire, and on his head were many crowns. A name was written on him that no one understood except himself. He wore a robe dipped in blood, and his title was the Word of God. From his mouth came a sharp sword to strike down the nations. He will rule them with an iron rod. He will release the fierce wrath of God, the Almighty, like juice flowing from a winepress. On his robe at his thigh was written this title: King of all kings and Lord of all lords"

(Revelation 19:11–16 NLT)

Chapter Twenty-One

God's Recognition Versus Man's Recognition

"Dear friends, don't be afraid of those who want to kill your body; they cannot do any more to you after that. But I'll tell you whom to fear. Fear God, who has the power to kill you and then throw you into hell. Yes, He's the one to fear"

(Luke 12:4–5 NLT)

I have always held the notion that those who preach on busy roads, either early in the morning or at any convenient time, are not likely to make the desired impact. Some time ago, I left my home at about 5:30 a.m. and just at the first corner of the street where I lived, a woman was preaching. As I drove past, I was still able to pick a part of her message, which was asking her listeners to be more interested in gaining recognition from God and less interested in gaining recognition from man. I once had the privilege of attending the burial ceremony of a prominent businessman. I knew him at reasonably close quarters, so I had a good idea of how he took the things of God. Like some wealthy people, he was committed to Christian charity but was far less committed to Christian living. Though it is not for me to judge him or any other person on that matter, what was of note was the way the ministers struggled to outdo each other in pouring encomiums on the departed businessman at his wake-keep and burial services. One minister even went to the extent of saying that he was certain that the man had scored more than 80 percent and that he was already with God in heaven. I did not need to check my Bible to see that no man will sit at God's judgment throne to judge others and that no matter the recognition we attract from man, even from ministers of God, it does not matter to God.

The recognition that man gives is limited in scope while that of God is unlimited. God's recognition is the better of the two, so all should go for it. The problem, however, is that man's recognition is more often glamorous, and just like the broad way to destruction, it is attractive and so many people opt for it.

God's recognition is sure and will come to those worthy of it. While the recognition that man offers is discretionary and temporary, God's recognition is indisputable and eternal. Heaven and earth may pass away, but God will not fail to fulfill His promises and reward all, using His standard.

Man's recognition may be misapplied, manipulated, or given to the wrong person. It can also be accorded in a quantum below or above the due of the recipient because of human error or sentiments, but God's recognition to

His children cannot be tampered with; it may wait a while, but it will certainly come as determined by Him.

Man's recognition may be influenced by the third party either for good or bad; it may also not be equitable. With God's recognition, recipient selection and type of reward is made by the Almighty Himself. No one else has a say. It cannot be manipulated, as what we sow we must reap.

There are many ways to gain man's recognition. It is a way that may seem right, but the end is destruction. God, on the other hand, offers recognition to only His friends— those who obey His commandments. It is therefore unwise to seek both man's and God's recognition at the same time. We must choose one.

Seeking after God's recognition is not rocket science. Joseph was a 17-year-old boy when he was sold into slavery, but he remained focused on gaining God's recognition, and he went to jail for it. Samuel was a prophet, who, like it is today, had the opportunity to exploit those who came to him for one thing or the other by virtue of his position. But because God's recognition was more important to him, he stood firm on his principles. Also, Nehemiah was a governor whose predecessors were trading influence for money, but because receiving God's recognition was paramount in his heart, he declined to go in that direction. Many of Jesus' disciples died as martyrs because they turned down man's recognition and opted for God's instead. Daniel and his three Hebrew friends had the option of trading God's recognition for friendship with the most powerful man in the world during their time, but they did not take it. Jesus also wanted His father's recognition, so instead of turning back at the garden of Gethsemane, He went to the Cross.

> *"No one here has more authority than I do. He has held back nothing from me except you because you are his wife. How could I do such a wicked thing? It would be a great sin against God"*
>
> *(Genesis 39:9 NLT)*

> *"'Now testify against me in the presence of the Lord and before His anointed one. Whose ox or donkey have I stolen? Have I ever cheated any of you? Have I ever oppressed you? Have I ever taken a bribe and perverted justice? Tell me, and I will make right whatever I have done wrong.' 'No,' they replied, 'you have never cheated or oppressed us, and you have never taken even a single bribe.' 'The Lord and His anointed one are my witnesses today,' Samuel declared, 'that my hands are clean.' 'Yes, he is a witness,' they replied"*
>
> *(1 Samuel 12:3–5 NLT)*

> *"For the entire twelve years that I was governor of Judah—from the twentieth year to the thirty-second year of the reign of King Artaxerxes—neither I nor my officials drew on our official food allowance. The former governors, in contrast, had laid heavy burdens*

on the people, demanding a daily ration of food and wine, besides forty pieces of silver. Even their assistants took advantage of the people. But because I feared God, I did not act that way"

(Nehemiah 5:14–15 NLT)

The ultimate recognition is to get a crown of righteousness when we die. This is the best, most perfect recognition that God can give anyone. It is available only to those who truly believe in Him and live their lives for Him.

I pray that always you will find the will to focus your attention on gaining God's recognition in Jesus' name.

Chapter Twenty-Two

Be A Shining Star For God

"You are the light of the world—like a city on a hilltop that cannot be hidden. No one lights a lamp and then puts it under a basket. Instead, a lamp is placed on a stand, where it gives light to everyone in the house. In the same way, let your good deeds shine out for all to see so that everyone will praise your heavenly Father"

(Matthew 5:14–16 NLT)

Lagos will undoubtedly pass as West Africa's commercial capital, maybe even sub-Saharan Africa's, though Johannesburg will have something to say about this claim. However, even if Lagos cannot beat Johannesburg at this title, it can certainly lay claim to a much higher population. It's a tough city to live in primarily because its infrastructure is creaking under the weight of its over 20 million inhabitants. On a Friday, as I was driving to work, and after close to one hour on the wheels, I began to wonder generally about life, my life. At the end of the short period of reflection while still on the wheels, a message of resolve dropped into my mind, and I said: I AM GOING TO BE A SHINING STAR FOR GOD.

In the Baptist Church where I grew up, we have several departments and units, all put together, to develop the members of the church spiritually. One of these bodies which are under the Women Missionary Union is the Sunbeam Band for boys and girls under ten years. The Sunbeam means ray of sunlight. This unit has an excellent theme song which defines the purpose of the group.

The Sunbeam member is taught in the song that Jesus wants him or her to be a shining light each day. They are trained to please God in every situation and place they find themselves. For the Sunbeam, loving others must be akin to second nature; they must show kindness at all times and to all. The song emphasizes to the little ones that all these good virtues only come from Jesus alone who helps them to be like Himself. Early in their lives, they are reminded that sin is to be hated with a passion and that the best way to reflect on the goodness of God and shine for him is always to turn their back to sin. At this very tender age, service is introduced even to the young ones as they focus early on how to reign with Christ.

> *"One day some parents brought their children to Jesus so He could lay His hands on them and pray for them. But the disciples scolded the parents for bothering him. But Jesus said, 'Let the children come to me. Don't stop them! For the Kingdom of Heaven belongs to those who are like these children.' And He placed His hands on their heads and blessed them before he left"*
>
> *(Matthew 19:13–15 NLT)*

Jesus Christ is the source of light. We cannot shine without Him. He is the Word that gave life to everything that was created, AND HIS LIFE BROUGHT LIGHT TO EVERYONE. The light that Jesus brings to your life can only shine through if there is no opaque object blocking it. That opaque object is the sin in our lives. Sin will not allow God's light to shine through your life. Light always overpowers darkness. Darkness has never won any contest with light, so light is the better choice for the wise. Jesus wants you to start shinning from childhood so that when you have reached adulthood, you will have become a shining star for your creator. Jesus wants your light to shine everywhere for all to see just like the sunbeam song says— at home, school, and play.

Light is a metaphor for holiness. Jesus is, therefore, saying to you that He wants you to distinguish yourself by shining in holiness. There is no other meaning of shining in the dictionary of your creator. Jesus shone in the world because no sin was found in Him (1 Peter 2: 22–23). He shone because that was His father's mandate given to Him to show you and I that it is possible to shine. You too, therefore, must go and do likewise. It is possible for you to shine brightly even as the morning star.

"Do everything without complaining and arguing, so that no one can criticize you. Live clean, innocent lives as children of God, shining like bright lights in a world full of crooked and perverse people"

(Philippians 2:14–15 NLT)

I pray that you will receive divine enablement to shine for your creator in Jesus' name. Amen.

Chapter Twenty-Three

What Is The Value Of Your Soul?

"Then, calling the crowd to join His disciples, He said, 'If any of you wants to be my follower, you must give up your own way, take up your cross, and follow me. If you try to hang on to your life, you will lose it. But if you give up your life for my sake and for the sake of the Good News, you will save it. And what do you benefit if you gain the whole world but lose your own soul? Is anything worth more than your soul? If anyone is ashamed of me and my message in these adulterous and sinful days, the Son of Man will be ashamed of that person when He returns in the glory of His Father with the holy angels'"

(Mark 8:34–38 NLT)

When people close to us pass away, it is not uncommon for us to think about eternity. I recently learned about the death of a young lawyer who was about 45 years old. He had met his untimely death at the hands of the men of the underworld. He was someone to whom I was connected, though I only spoke to him a few times on the phone. I recently heard of another man who held a prominent position in a publicly quoted company and who lost his life aged below 40 years. In the second instance, he had reported to hospital feeling unwell, and between the time of admission and his spouse's return with items required for his hospital stay, he was no more. Another friend and classmate also lost his life when he suddenly collapsed and died. He had had a typical day teaching and attending to patients in a hospital. He was only in his 50's. The fact that all humanity must face death is incontrovertible: some at infancy, some at middle age, and others at old age. No one has been known to escape it. I often reflect on life with this reality in mind—and it is good to do so. However, the most important thing is what comes out of our reflection. Some reflect on making the right decision while others daydream and waste time until death comes to them.

I see the value of a soul in two very short parables that Jesus told His disciples. In the hidden treasure and choice pearl parables, there was a concerted effort by the man in the two stories to trade off everything he owned to gain the asset in question. This is the wise thing to do or best example to follow when it comes to the safety of an asset as valuable as your soul.

> *"The Kingdom of Heaven is like a treasure that a man discovered hidden in a field. In his excitement, he hid it again and sold everything he owned to get enough money to buy the field. Again, the Kingdom of Heaven is like a merchant on the lookout for choice pearls. When he discovered a pearl of great value, he sold everything he owned and bought it!"*
>
> *(Matthew 13:44–46 NLT)*

What is the value of your soul? Are you prepared to sacrifice everything you own to save your soul from destruction? Or would you instead choose to gain the whole world and lose your soul?

Jesus asked a question during His time which is still pertinent today. IS ANYTHING WORTH MORE THAN YOUR SOUL? You need to answer this question even today.

Don't just think about your today but think more about your eternity! I pray that you will open the door of your heart to Jesus who is the only one that can save your soul from destruction.

Chapter Twenty-Four

There Is Hope For The Righteous

"But Caleb tried to quiet the people as they stood before Moses. 'Let's go at once to take the land,' he said. 'We can certainly conquer it!'"

(Numbers 13:30 NLT)

Sunday is usually one of my best days of the week. The day comes with the certainty that the time spent in the presence of God will be invaluable. It's always a time of renewal. No wonder David said; "I was glad when they said unto me, let us go into the house of the Lord."

On a particular Saturday, I traveled out of Lagos and because of the road construction taking place on the Lagos-Ibadan Expressway, I was on the road for a total of 570 minutes—nine and a half hours behind the steering wheel. I was dead tired by the time I came back home, and it began to cross my mind that I should not attend any of the services on Sunday. By the time I went to bed, I had resolved that instead of missing both services, it would be better to attend the second service which comes up much later. As God would have it, I slept early and woke up soon enough to attend the first service, though I was a bit late. The message God sent to us, delivered through one of our

Deacons, was titled "Divine visitation." Although he took his lesson from the very popular Bible story of Jesus healing at the pool of Bethesda, it was the concluding part of his message which focused on how to attract divine visitation that stayed longer in my mind.

> *"Righteousness exalts a nation, but sin condemns any people"*
>
> *(Proverbs 14:34 NIV)*

> *"Whoever pursues righteousness and love finds life, prosperity, and honor"*
>
> *(Proverbs 21:21 NIV)*

> *"The eyes of the Lord are on the righteous, and His ears are attentive to their cry"*
>
> *(Psalm 34:15 NIV)*

Nigeria, like most third world countries, is infested with leadership-induced poverty and misery. It is, therefore, not uncommon for most to want to "help" themselves by getting involved in all manner of evil and ungodly practices. Many no longer believe that it is possible to live to please God and so proceed to take matters into their own hands thinking that is the only way available to make ends meet. But there are still many others who have remained faithful, retaining their allegiance to righteousness and Godly living. You, too, can be one of them. As was the case in times past, God's children still wait on Him, and He never disappoints.

"He replied again, 'I have zealously served the Lord God Almighty. But the people of Israel have broken their covenant with you, torn down your altars, and killed every one of your prophets. I am the only one left, and now they are trying to kill me, too. Yet I will preserve 7,000 others in Israel who have never bowed down to Baal or kissed him!'"

(1 Kings 19:14, 18)

God is reassuring us again in today's message that notwithstanding our situation if we play our part, He is faithful and true to His words.

The testimonies in the lives of Joshua and Caleb prove that God is ready to honor His words no matter what the circumstances are and no matter what it will take to keep His promise. The obstacles to their entry to the Promised Land were real and not imagined, but God is bigger than all our problems. Ten others confirmed this to be true, but the righteous have a different life pattern, and these two followed it to the letter.

"For in the gospel, the righteousness of God is revealed—a righteousness that is by faith from first to last, just as it is written: 'The righteous will live by faith'"

(Romans 1:17 NIV)

The faith of Joshua and Caleb inspired the song below:

"We are able to go up and take the country,

To possess the land from Jordan to the sea.

Though the giant may be on the way to hinder,

God will surely give us victory. VICTORY!

Move on to the righteous side,

Move on to the righteous side,

Move on to the righteous side of God. Hallelujah!"

The key to overcoming your life's challenge is to adopt a righteous lifestyle so that God will be involved in your situation. There is hope for you if you turn to God today. There is indeed hope for the righteous.

I know that God will give you testimonies when you provoke Him with righteous living. I plead with you to move on to the righteous side. God is expecting you on His side.

Chapter Twenty-Five

Before It Is Too Late

"Seek the Lord while you can find Him. Call on Him now while He is near. Let the wicked change their ways and banish the very thought of doing wrong. Let them turn to the Lord that He may have mercy on them. Yes, turn to our God, for He will forgive generously"

(Isaiah 55:6–7 NLT)

In late August 2018, the world woke up to the news of the impending arrival of a life-threatening storm, nicknamed Hurricane Florence, which was set to hit North Carolina in the United States of America. The U.S., not being new to these kinds of natural disasters, quickly braced itself, with authorities and citizens preparing for every eventuality and many following the government's advice to leave town. As I write, Florence has already made landfall, leaving no one in doubt that it meant business, which is to wreak as much havoc as possible. Up until its arrival, the news networks, both local and international, tried to outdo each other with updates, especially as they relate to preparation for the inevitable. The president and the state governor both made the danger ahead very clear and warned of the need to act wisely by preferably getting out of town. Later in the week,

I saw a video clip on one of the major U.S. news networks showing a gridlock of different vehicles all moving out of the city. Earlier in the week, many were seen buying extra food, supplies, gasoline, and even generators in advance of the storm. Others tried to prepare their homes, to the best of their ability, to withstand the storm. Trust Americans, even in the midst of problems, to make a big show of it.

Florence finally made its arrival, knocking out power in more than 600,000 homes, causing buildings to crumble, and stranding residents. Wind speed was at 150 kilometers per hour with heavy rainfall. Lives have also been reported lost.

As I reflected on the Hurricane Florence saga, I could not help but be reminded that there is an event of far greater significance and consequence taking place very soon whose certainty of occurrence is far surer than that of this hurricane. It is the greatest day of reckoning in the history of humanity. It's a day that will make Hurricane Florence seem like child's play to those who are not prepared for it. Many who live in North Carolina have done the wise thing by getting out of town before it is too late. Others have stayed behind, fortifying themselves one way or the other. Unfortunately, so many of these people and others not facing the dangers of Florence are not preparing for this massive day of reckoning that will soon befall the whole world.

On the day of reckoning, a trumpet shall sound, and it will be heard all over the world at the same time, and then Jesus Christ will appear. It will be the end of the world, and when this happens everyone will subsequently be made to face the judgment throne of God. Everyone will be made to give an account of how he or she has lived his or her life. On this day, there will be no more opportunity to right any wrong. It will, indeed, be a day of enormous reckoning.

> *"Sound the trumpet in Jerusalem! Raise the alarm on my holy mountain! Let everyone tremble in fear because the day of the Lord is upon us. It is a day of darkness and gloom, a day of thick clouds and deep blackness. Suddenly, like dawn spreading across the mountains, a great and mighty army appears. Nothing like it has been seen before or will ever be seen again"*
>
> *(Joel 2:1–2 NLT)*

Dearly beloved, the arrival of Hurricane Florence at the southeastern coastline of the U.S. is an example of the TERRIFYING THINGS Jesus gave as end-time signs and is proof that He is coming soon. He has already warned that such events would herald His second coming, so while you prepare for such calamities or sympathize with those who experience it, please remember that what is most important is for you to be ready for when Jesus will come back again.

"There will be great earthquakes, and there will be famines and plagues in many lands, and there will be terrifying things and great miraculous signs from heaven"

(Luke 21:11 NLT)

I pray that when Jesus comes back to reward His servants, He will find you watching, waiting, and worthy. I want to appeal to you that if you still live your life without a relationship with Jesus, today is another opportunity to redress this anomaly. Jesus is tenderly calling on you today.

Author's Contact Information

@   oyewo611@yahoo.co.uk
      souls4christ@hodm.com.ng

f   adeoye oyewo

   @adeoyeoyewo

   @adeoyeoyewo

   +2348034022617

9 781612 447148